UNLEASHING
The Gospel of Christ

THE TRUTH IS NOT CONFINED
TO MAN'S REASONING

D.L. FULLER

Charleston, SC
www.PalmettoPublishing.com

Unleashing The Gospel of Christ

Copyright © 2020 by D. L. Fuller

Cover art by Jah'son Fuller.

ISBN-13: 978-1-64990-334-1
ISBN-10: 1-64990-334-0

TABLE OF CONTENTS

THE INTRODUCTION

After Adam and Eve lost their faith in GOD, they also lost their access to the tree of life. Now, by the grace and mercy of YAHWEH, the tree of life has been put back within the reach of everyone who will believe in His love again. The tree of Life came to us in the flesh and called for all men to eat His flesh and drink His blood.

51 I am the living bread which came down from heaven: if any man eat of this bread, he shall live for ever: and the bread that I will give is my flesh, which I will give for the life of the world.

52 The Jews therefore strove among themselves, saying, How can this man give us his flesh to eat?

53 Then Jesus said unto them, Verily, verily, I say unto you, Except ye eat the flesh of the Son of man, and drink his blood, ye have no life in you. 54 Whoso eateth my flesh, and drinketh my blood, hath eternal life; and I will raise him up at the last day. 55 For my flesh is meat indeed, and my blood is drink indeed. 56 He that eateth my flesh, and drinketh my blood, dwelleth in me, and I in him. 57 As the living Father hath sent me, and I live by the Father: so he that eateth me, even he shall live by me." (John 6:51-57 KJV)

We read in the first chapter of the book of John that the WORD of YAHWEH became flesh and dwelt on earth, so eating His flesh is symbolic of internalizing the WORD of GOD.

¹In the beginning was the Word, and the Word was with God, and the Word was God. ² The same was in the beginning with God. ³ All things were made by him; and without him was not any thing made that was made. ⁴ In him was life; and the life was the light of men. ⁵ And the light shineth in darkness; and the darkness comprehended it not." (John 1:1-5 KJV)

¹⁰ He was in the world, and the world was made by him, and the world knew him not. ¹¹ He came unto his own, and his own received him not. ¹² But as many as received him, to them gave he power to become the sons of God, even to them that believe on his name: ¹³ Which were born, not of blood, nor of the will of the flesh, nor of the will of man, but of God. ¹⁴ And the Word was made flesh, and dwelt among us, (and we beheld his glory, the glory as of the only begotten of the Father,) full of grace and truth. (John 1:10-14 KJV)

We are to consume the WORD with our faith and belief. As we immerse our heart and mind into the WORD, the WORD fills us, so we abide in the WORD and the WORD abides in us. We abandon our own ways and our own thoughts, our life, for the life that is in the WORD, and we know the WORD is none other the YESHUA HAMASHIACH (Jesus the Christ), which came down from heaven. As we are joined with the life of YESHUA, we become alive as the children of GOD, born of His will. This is the salvation of GOD; the way He has provided to redeem man from the death of disobedience. Those born of GOD through the life of YESHUA live according to the nature of GOD in righteousness because they are of Him.

Whosoever is born of God doth not commit sin; for his seed remaineth in him: and he cannot sin, because he is born of God. (1 John 3:9 KJV)

This is the gospel of Christ. As rare as it is preached, as impossible as it may seem, this is the true gospel. Salvation is an impossible proposition for man. That is why it begins at the cross, where we surrender trying to save ourselves and commit to daily getting out of GOD's way, so He can perform the work. Through the simplicity of belief and trust, as little children trust their parents, we have been called to follow GOD into The WAY everlasting. The truth challenges everything untrue and ingenuine. We must be ready to abandon any beliefs, thoughts, traditions, or behaviors not founded on truth, for the reality that is in GOD and that is GOD. YESHUA came with the sword of the spirit to divide between the true and the false, light and darkness, good and evil, His works and the works of the devil. It is through the light in His life that we are freed from darkness to clearly choose life.

Unfortunately, much of what I hear today from professing Christians isn't what is written in the record of His word. Today, the gospel of Christ is constantly being interpreted from hearts adulterated with the love of this present world and unbelief. The impact is a church void of the glorious light and life of Christ. I have written this book in the sincere belief that GOD is able to do all He has promised, and that He specializes in performing what man sees as impossible, for His glory unto the salvation of souls. My sincere hope is that this book will serve as a sword of the spirit, which illuminates the gospel of Christ unto revival of His life in the Church for the redeeming of the lost and for the perfecting of the saints, and for the edifying of the body of Christ.

CHAPTER 1
THE FEAR OF THE LORD

Proverbs 1:7 (KJV) reads:

The fear of the Lord is the beginning of knowledge: but fools despise wisdom and instruction.

Psalm 111:10 (KJV) reads:

The fear of the Lord is the beginning of wisdom: a good understanding have all they that do his commandments: his praise endureth for ever.

Proverbs 2:4–6 (KJV) reads:

If thou seekest her as silver, and searchest for her as for hid treasures; Then shalt thou understand the fear of the Lord, and find the knowledge of God. For the Lord giveth wisdom: out of his mouth cometh knowledge and understanding.

The fear of the Lord is the frame that holds the picture of GOD. You cannot begin to understand the first things of GOD until you have a frame of reference from which to approach His Gloriousness. Without the framing of the fear of the Lord, you will lack the proper perspective to prioritize even the most miniscule things of GOD. It is easy for someone not understanding the fear of the Lord to forsake some detail of GOD as trivial, not realizing it will tip the scale and unbalance their life.

Verse 25 in chapter 1 of 1 Corinthians (KJV) reads:

Because the foolishness of God is wiser than men; and the weakness of God is stronger than men.

The fear of the Lord teaches you your place in respect to the one by which all things are sustained. The whole of creation is the product of His brilliance, and all things have purpose according to His design. This is why it is of vital importance to understand the correct order of things, to avoid vanity, perversion, and destruction.

The Lord YESHUA explains in John 14:6 (KJV), *"I am the way, the truth, and the life."* GOD is reality. Anything outside of GOD is mere deception and not real at all. To seek GOD is to seek life. When you are seeking GOD, you are seeking all things, because He is the beginning and conclusion of all things that are real. When you have the right perspective from the fear of the Lord, you understand that the knowledge and wisdom of GOD is the key to enjoying creation to the fullest. Those unlearned in the fear of the Lord seek creation more than the creator and squander the intended blessings of creation. GOD made creation so good that even its misuse brings a small level of enjoyment. I say "a small level" because the shallow enjoyment experienced through unenlightened experimentation is nothing compared to the deep fulfillment experienced by those instructed in the fear of the Lord, who have humbled themselves to live according to the Creator's design. When true purpose is fulfilled, the experience is optimized. The fulfillment of the soul is made possible by the enlightenment of the spirit. In order to save the world, YESHUA came to restore that light.

The book of John begins with a teaching on the fear of the Lord. It reads,

> *¹ In the beginning was the Word, and the Word was with God, and the Word was God. ² The same was in the beginning with God. ³ All things were made by him; and without him was not any thing made that was made. ⁴ In him was life; and the life was the light of men.* (John 1:1–4 KJV).

The fear of the Lord is the first illumination. Once you begin to understand creation after the fear of the Lord, then instruction can begin. There is no randomness about creation. Everything fits together according to a specific design and function. There is definite order and relationship in creation. Creation tells us many things about the Creator, because creation is an expression of the Creator. Creation is even reflective of the Creator. One could no more dismiss the relationship between a piece of art and the mind of an artist, than creation from the mind of the Creator. Unfortunately, people who don't understand the fear of the Lord make this mistake every day.

Though creation is specific, ordered, and intentional, many unenlightened people speak of the Almighty GOD as if He is actually many different things to many different people, instead of someone specific, with an order, and distinct. The problem here is that people define GOD as they see fit, instead of humbling themselves to accept GOD's definition of Himself. The hidden motive of the rebellious and prideful is to allow room for them to define themselves, instead of humbling themselves to conform to GOD's definition of them. This is at the root of why people use anamorphic names like "the man upstairs" and "my higher power" to refer to their deity. I say "their deity," because actually they aren't referring to the Almighty at all. They are actually referring to the deity in their mind, which they have concocted, that fits their way of living. People may not actively seek out forgers of metal and carvers of wood to custom design their deities any longer, but people very much still form images in their mind of a god they are comfortable with, and make that image their deity. You can easily have in the same room a Mormon, a Ku Klux Klan member, a homosexual, a Jehovah Witness, a Seventh-day Adventist, a

Catholic priest, and a transvestite who all confess that they know GOD and serve Him. This conundrum is due to an overall lack in understanding the fear of the Lord. Conforming to the universal standards and principles of the Creator is more important and vital than conforming to individual appetites and ambitions. The fear of the Lord teaches that instead of defaming the character, nature, and image of GOD to comply with the preferences of any one person or group, we must humbly conform to the one true and living GOD. This is what YESHUA spoke of when He said:

> *If any man will come after me, let him deny himself, and take up his cross, and follow me."* (Matthew 16:24 KJV)

It is also what YESHUA is referring to when He says:

> *For whosoever will save his life shall lose it: and whosoever will lose his life for my sake shall find it."* (Matthew 16:25 KJV)

The fear of the Lord teaches that God is life, and we should seek our existence in Him, for outside of God there is only death. Anything that opposes God inherently opposes life, and should be considered evil. Proverbs 8:13 (KJV) says:

> *The fear of the Lord is to hate evil: pride, and arrogancy, and the evil way, and the froward mouth, do I hate."*

Pride and arrogance should be hated, because those characteristics support and strengthen self-reliance, instead of reliance on GOD. Many people object to the view that we should fear a loving GOD. Those who feel this way often say the Bible is only referring to a reverential fear, and not a sense of terror. Rejecting the concept that we should actually fear GOD, based on the idea the word "fear" in the phrase "the fear of the Lord" was mistranslated, is evil in root—evil because it refuses to surrender its humanistic ideas of GOD. GOD Himself says we should dread opposing Him, and scripture strongly supports that there is virtue in fearing GOD. It is very true that GOD is a loving GOD, but it is also true that GOD will recompense evil. GOD hates evil, and regularly destroys it. The Almighty GOD is terrible and fearful. He is not one to be played with or provoked. The Apostle Paul says in Hebrews 10:31 (KJV), *"It is a fearful thing to fall into the hands of the living God."* In Hebrews, chapter 10, Paul is trying to make sure that we do not forsake the fear of the Lord in this dispensation of amazing grace, after the sacrifice of Christ. Paul is warning us not to take GOD for granted, as if GOD is going to remit the sins we continue to commit willingly, after we know better. YESHUA taught in Matthew 10:28 (KJV):

Fear not them which kill the body, but are not able to kill the soul: but rather fear him which is able to destroy both soul and body in hell.

This is New Testament teaching on the Fear of the Lord by God Himself. Proverbs 16:6 (KJV) says:

By mercy and truth iniquity is purged: and by the fear of the Lord men depart from evil.

Through the mercies of GOD, truth is revealed. There is a lot of preparing of the heart that takes place by the hand of GOD before the truth is sown, much like a farmer prepares the earth for a crop he wants to harvest. The fear of the Lord restrains men from evil, which keeps them alive while the truth takes root, and the iniquity is purged. It is the fear of the Lord that makes man teachable. It is my hope that the teachings of this book will build upon your foundation of the fear of the Lord, toward a deeper and more fulfilling relationship with GOD.

CHAPTER 2
MEET THE SAVIOR

"1 The Spirit of the Lord God is upon Me,

Because the Lord has anointed Me

To preach good tidings to the poor;

He has sent Me to heal the brokenhearted,

To proclaim liberty to the captives,

And the opening of the prison to those who are bound;

2 To proclaim the acceptable year of the Lord,

And the day of vengeance of our God;

To comfort all who mourn,

³ To console those who mourn in Zion,

To give them beauty for ashes,

The oil of joy for mourning,

The garment of praise for the spirit of heaviness;

That they may be called trees of righteousness,

The planting of the Lord, that He may be glorified." (Isaiah 61:1-3 NKJV)

That was the prophecy given to Isaiah from YAHWEH to describe YESHUA HAMASHIACH, interpreted Jesus the Messiah. This was the same block of scripture that YESHUA read in the temple when He proclaimed, *"This day is this prophecy fulfilled,"* confirming His identity as The Anointed One or The Christ.

If you recognize yourself as poor, He came for you.

If you feel your heart is broken, He came for you.

If you feel you are being held captive, marginalized, and oppressed, He came for you.

If you feel you are being restrained from experiencing the fullness of life, and barriers have been set around you, He came for you.

He came to let you know that now is the time of your liberation and now is the time to throw down your enemies. Now is the time for you to be comforted and consoled. Now is the time for you to exchange your shamefacedness with beauty. Now is the time to replace your wailing with rejoicing. Now it is time to replace all the reasons to mourn with reasons to give thanks.

Once you allow Christ to perform these operations in your life, then you will be identified as a tree of righteousness, even His own planting, that He might be glorified, and that others might see and welcome Him. Psalms 23 gives us an idea of how He will bring all this to pass.

¹ The Lord is my shepherd; I shall not want.

² He makes me to lie down in green pastures;

He leads me beside the still waters.

³ He restores my soul;

He leads me in the paths of righteousness

For His name's sake.

⁴ Yea, though I walk through the valley of the shadow of death,

I will fear no evil;

For You are with me;

Your rod and Your staff, they comfort me.

⁵ You prepare a table before me in the presence of my enemies;

You anoint my head with oil;

My cup runs over.

⁶ Surely goodness and mercy shall follow me

All the days of my life;

And I will dwell in the house of the Lord

Forever. (Psalms 23 NKJV)

Let YESHUA become your Shepherd. Make a determination to follow Him, wherever He leads. You may say, "If I could see Him, I certainly would." You must understand that He and His words are one. When you follow His words, you are following Him. Gaze into the Bible, just as you would gaze into His face, and follow His words as you would follow His steps.

You may not be able to see the miracles, which Christ performed in the past, but through studying His words, you will be able to see His heart, and that will open your eyes to the miracles He is performing today. My life is one of those nowadays miracles.

GOD is known throughout the Bible for His miraculous ability to draw an abundance out of nothing or very little. I was born to a brown-skinned, single, teenage woman in the racist south, not even a year after the U.S. passed the Voting Rights Act. For those unfamiliar with America's racist history, the Voting Rights Act was passed in order to make it illegal for states to continue the practice of hindering Black people from voting. If states in the U.S. found Black people undeserving of the right to vote, you can imagine what other rights and privileges of citizenship were being withheld. My earthly father has been absent from my life. The absence of his strength and guidance increased the deficits of a life already impoverished. Though my earthly father and I have lived in the same state, we have spoken on very few occasions, totaling maybe ninety minutes throughout my entire life. I love him and have no ill feelings toward him; however, it is evident that his values do not count a relationship with me or his grandchildren worthy of the cost. I made it clear to him in a conversation when I was twenty-one, that I had been fathered by GOD, and I considered him free from any indebtedness he may have felt he owed me. I spent the first years of my life in the University Housing Projects for Negroes, in Atlanta, Georgia. Not my words—that is what the housing projects were called. I consider these to be humble beginnings, though I know there are many who have come from far less.

Here are a few of the ways YESHUA's miracle of abundance and grace has touched my life. Never having a man to model for me how to be a husband or a father, I have been married for over thirty years to the mother of our four children, all born from the sanctity of our unity in marriage. I feel very blessed to have fathered four children who are healthy and intelligent and are all seeking their lives through a relationship with GOD.

I began my life being cared for by women on government welfare assistance to providing for my wife and children on a six-figure salary as an IT professional. To be clear, I am not boasting of my accomplishments; I am boasting of the miraculous power and ability of YESHUA the Christ to bring an abundance from very little. He has already exceeded my expectations, and He isn't done yet. He took a little boy who had no clue what it meant to be a man and enabled him to honor the request of five grooms to be their "Best Man." I like to think I am like the boy in the book of John 6:9, who surrendered his two fish and five loaves of bread and through the power of YESHUA was able to feed a multitude. In my personal instance of this miracle, I had even less than the little boy from John 6:9; however, I have faith that YESHUA will feed even more as I share the bread of Life.

I have never been to Mount Sinai where Moses encountered GOD, nor have I been to the Mount of Olives where many witnessed Christ giving the Word of Life, but I testify that the Love of GOD, which transcends space and time, has personally touched my heart and continues to as promised in John 14:23 (KJV);

Jesus answered and said unto him, If a man love me, he will keep my words: and my Father will love him, and we will come unto him, and make our abode with him.

The Savior is still fulfilling the prophecy of Isaiah 61:1-3. He will meet you right where you are if you call on Him in sincerity of heart. He is not a respecter of persons; we are all His favorite. If you have not met the Savior of the Most High GOD, pray to Him today. The prayer that YESHUA gave us will serve well.

⁹ After this manner therefore pray ye: Our Father which art in heaven, Hallowed be thy name. ¹⁰ Thy kingdom come, Thy will be done in earth, as it is in heaven. ¹¹ Give us this day our daily bread. ¹² And forgive us our debts, as we forgive our debtors. ¹³ And lead us not into temptation, but deliver us from evil: For thine is the kingdom, and the power, and the glory, for ever. Amen. (Matthew 6:9-13 KJV)

CHAPTER 3
THE TRUTH ABOUT SIN

I have learned that people will suffer a lot for what they love. I look at what Olympic athletes put themselves through in order to stand on that podium or likewise any athlete looking to be crowned champion. I look at what women go through in pregnancy to build a family. I look at the politics and corporate bureaucracy, which men and women endure in order to provide for their families. If a person holds a sincere belief that something promises a worthy reward, they will endure a lot to obtain it.

Christ states plainly that in this life we will have tribulations.

These things I have spoken unto you, that in me ye might have peace. In the world ye shall have tribulation: but be of good cheer; I have overcome the world. (John 16:33 KJV)

In the verse above, YESHUA is referring to the persecution, which comes from living righteously in a wicked world. On the other hand, the Bible speaks at length about the inevitable pain and suffering, which follows living wickedly as well. This may sound like a darned if you do or darned if you don't scenario, but that depends on what you love and believe. It is your belief about what you seek which determines what you are willing to sacrifice to obtain it. Our actions tell us the truth about what we believe and love. This is what YESHUA was speaking to in Matthew 5:29-30. (NKJV)

> *29 If your right eye causes you to sin, pluck it out and cast it from you; for it is more profitable for you that one of your members perish, than for your whole body to be cast into hell. 30 And if your right hand causes you to sin, cut it off and cast it from you; for it is more profitable for you that one of your members perish, than for your whole body to be cast into hell.*

YESHUA wasn't just being mean; He was being a wonderful counselor and revealing the hearts of those who listened to themselves. In other words, if you truly love me as you profess, what are you willing to sacrifice in order to be with me in Heaven? Don't misunderstand me, Christ definitely feels it is that important, and He gave His own life to demonstrate to us how much He loves us. What He is causing us to ponder are our own actions, and what they say about what we value, love, and truly believe. YESHUA walks in spirit and in truth, and His actions are in direct agreement with what He professes. On the other hand, many Christians are still carnal and live in deception, and their actions are not in alignment with what they profess. The scripture in Hebrews 12:2-4 (KJV) calls us to accept the truth about this.

> *2 Looking unto Jesus the author and finisher of our faith; who for the joy that was set before him endured the cross, despising the shame, and is set down at the right hand of the throne of God. 3 For consider him that endured such contradiction of sinners against himself, lest ye be wearied and faint in your minds. 4 Ye have not yet resisted unto blood, striving against sin.*

There have been many martyrs for the gospel of Christ, and I can tell you with confidence that they were not struggling with rebellion against GOD. No one willing to give their very life for the Word of GOD and the faith is going to practice sin, which is rebellion against GOD.

Here is how sin is defined:

Therefore to him that knoweth to do good, and doeth it not, to him it is sin. (James 4:17 KJV)

Forasmuch then as Christ hath suffered for us in the flesh, arm yourselves likewise with the same mind: for he that hath suffered in the flesh hath ceased from sin;" (1 Peter 4:1 KJV)

See, it doesn't take amputation— just true love and belief, and a willingness to persevere through a little suffering. I don't use the term "little" to marginalize your hardships. It is just that when I juxtapose the rewards of a relationship with GOD and living in Heaven, against the suffering required to obtain it, the suffering comes out small. This is what the Apostle Paul is writing about in Philippians 3:8 (NKJV),

Yea doubtless, and I count all things but loss for the excellency of the knowledge of Christ Jesus my Lord: for whom I have suffered the loss of all things, and do count them but dung, that I may win Christ.

So then, a struggle with sin is really a struggle with belief and values. This is why just telling someone that they will go to hell if they don't stop sinning is inadequate to lead them to righteousness. Hell is only as real as Heaven. If a person doesn't believe the reality of Heaven, there is no fire in hell for them either. Sin is powerful enough to muffle a guilty conscience, but nothing in earth will keep a person from what they deeply love and believe. It is a matter of if our hearts have been awakened to truly love. The effect of the gospel of Christ reaching the heart and being held in belief resurrects real Love in the heart. This is the teaching of Christ in John 14:21 (NKJV).

He who has My commandments and keeps them, it is he who loves Me. And he who loves Me will be loved by My Father, and I will love him and manifest Myself to him.

A heart that is broken can't hold anything, which leads to an unquenchable thirst and unrest which breeds, lust, greed, and bitterness. Only Christ can heal a broken heart because He is the one that created hearts in the first place. This is part of the mission of YESHUA HAMASHIACH, which nothing or no one else can do.

> *¹⁷And there was delivered unto him the book of the prophet Esaias. And when he had opened the book, he found the place where it was written, ¹⁸ The Spirit of the Lord is upon me, because he hath anointed me to preach the gospel to the poor; he hath sent me to heal the brokenhearted, to preach deliverance to the captives, and recovering of sight to the blind, to set at liberty them that are bruised, ¹⁹ To preach the acceptable year of the Lord. ²⁰ And he closed the book, and he gave it again to the minister, and sat down. And the eyes of all them that were in the synagogue were fastened on him. ²¹ And he began to say unto them, This day is this scripture fulfilled in your ears. (Luke 4:17-21)*

If someone else could have done it, then it wouldn't have been His mission. This scripture relates to a prophecy from the book of Isaiah, which spoke specifically of YESHUA HAMASHIACH.

Since sin is tied to a broken heart, then discipline and fear are not sufficient alone to remove sin from our lives. What I hope to be showing here is that sin is the result of not fully receiving the gifts of Christ in love. It isn't the power of the carnal nature that holds men captive to sin: it is the gravity of the black hole in men's heart. Only Christ can mend and fill a man's heart. That is what Christ is proclaiming when He says:

> *If the Son therefore shall make you free, ye shall be free indeed.* (John 8:36 KJV)

Therefore, if the servants of Christ will proclaim the gospel of Christ fully and unadulterated, then people have a much greater chance of being made free. This is what Romans 1:16 is all about.

For I am not ashamed of the gospel of Christ: for it is the power of God unto salvation to every one that believeth; to the Jew first, and also to the Greek. For therein is the righteousness of God revealed from faith to faith: as it is written, The just shall live by faith. (Romans1:16 KJV)

Faith in GOD is generated and sustained through the knowledge of His love.

⁴⁴ How can ye believe, which receive honour one of another, and seek not the honour that cometh from God only? ⁴⁵ Do not think that I will accuse you to the Father: there is one that accuseth you, even Moses, in whom ye trust. ⁴⁶ For had ye believed Moses, ye would have believed me; for he wrote of me. ⁴⁷ But if ye believe not his writings, how shall ye believe my words? (John 5:44-47 KJV)

They trusted that Moses was indeed a man used of GOD; however, they didn't have faith in his writings. They understood the underlying virtues of the law but couldn't apprehend the fullness of what Moses wrote in relationship to the testimony of GOD from Adam to YESHUA HAMASHIACH. Their hardened hearts prevented them from perceiving the undercurrent of YAHWEH's everlasting love flowing in the record of holy scripture, which are testimonies of all those who had come before and bore record of His acts. What will it take to receive this everlasting love from YAHWEH? Belief.

CHAPTER 4
TRUE BELIEF

The prayer of salvation…Wow, Romans 10:9 has to be one of the most misunderstood scriptures in the New Testament. I say that primarily because it is used so often.

> *That if thou shalt confess with thy mouth the Lord Jesus, and shalt believe in thine heart that God hath raised him from the dead, thou shalt be saved.* (Romans 10:9 KJV)

This scripture wasn't written to be a template for the prayer of salvation. It was written to describe the belief necessary to receive salvation. Verse ten explains that true belief leads a person to righteousness, and righteousness is faith in GOD's word. The Word says you must deny yourself and follow YESHUA to be saved. To deny yourself means to bring your flesh into subjection to the spirit of GOD. The cross is where YESHUA surrendered His life to save mankind. It is also where we are called to surrender our lives in exchange for His life. As a person cannot grab anything new if their hands are already full, this requirement of letting go of our lives is paramount in the transaction of salvation. Much misunderstanding surrounds accepting salvation because this part of the salvation requirement is often omitted or under emphasized. The result of this omission is that many people are proclaiming they are saved because they have recited Romans 10:9, but since they have not surrendered their carnal life on the cross, they are still in bondage to carnal living, therefore still ruled by sin. If you are still ruled by sin, then you are not saved. Take a look at Romans 8:13 (KJV):

> *For if ye live after the flesh, ye shall die: but if ye through the Spirit do mortify the deeds of the body, ye shall live.*

If the children of Israel were still in Egypt, under the scourge of Pharaoh, would they be saved? Nope.

This is a classic example of the blind leading the blind, or the carnal leading the carnal. Revival in the church must be preceded by a revival in the word of the spirit. All the carnal teaching in the church must cease. Carnal teaching may translate into a large number of members and the appearance of a successful church, but it doesn't please GOD.

I listened to a brother teach today, who had a master's degree in theology. Some of his doctrinal stances were just unfounded in scripture. One of the things he taught was that people are saved by confessing their belief in Christ, whether there was fruit of that belief or not. He simply believes, if you make a profession of faith in Christ then you are saved. Even if you live in sin until your last breath, your profession of belief has saved you. This is the kind of teaching, which undermines the true faith of Christ and works against the mighty deliverance wrought by the cross. One of the central accomplishments of the cross of Christ is new life.

> *What shall we say then? Shall we continue in sin that grace may abound? [2] Certainly not! How shall we who died to sin live any longer in it? [3] Or do you not know that as many of us as were baptized into Christ Jesus were baptized into His death? [4] Therefore we were buried with Him through baptism into death, that just as Christ was raised from the dead by the glory of the Father, even so we also should walk in newness of life.*

⁵ For if we have been united together in the likeness of His death, certainly we also shall be in the likeness of His resurrection, ⁶ knowing this, that our old man was crucified with Him, that the body of sin might be done away with, that we should no longer be slaves of sin. ⁷ For he who has died has been freed from sin. (Romans 6:1-7 NKJV)

Because of the misunderstanding of these scriptures in Romans, the Salvation of Christ is often mis-taught, which perpetuates the misunderstanding. There are many people who believe once you are saved, you are always saved. They mistakenly limit redemption to a paying of a fine. We are being saved from death. Death is the result of being disconnected from GOD, who is life. The only way a person can become saved and remain saved is by being reconnected to GOD and then staying connected. Abolishing the law by satisfying its requirements forever frees us from sentencing under the law, but it does not make us capable of a relationship with GOD. The only thing that makes us capable of having a healthy relationship with GOD is the ability to relate to Him. A healthy relationship is a union, which produces life. This is the true work of salvation, the work of transformation into His likeness, so that we are what He is. Salvation is the gift of the life of YESHUA HAMASHIACH, which quickens to life every man who surrenders his own life on the cross. By taking up our cross daily through denying carnal life the power to rule us again, we allow the life of Christ to consume us until we are completely like Him. Our salvation is contingent upon us staying the course and running the race until the end, that is taking up the cross daily and yielding to the work of the Holy Spirit, the life of Christ.

²⁴ Know ye not that they which run in a race run all, but one receiveth the prize? So run, that ye may obtain. ²⁵ And every man that striveth for the mastery is temperate in all things. Now they do it to obtain a corruptible crown; but we an incorruptible. ²⁶ I therefore so run, not as uncertainly; so fight I, not as one that beateth the air: ²⁷ But I keep under my body, and bring it into subjection: lest that by any means, when I have preached to others, I myself should be a castaway. (1 Corinthians 9:24-27 KJV)

The word "castaway" in this block of scripture comes from the Greek word *adokimos*, which means unapproved or rejected. We don't want to be as the Apostle Paul says, "as one which beateth the air," competing outside of the rules only to find ourselves disqualified at the end. We must run this race according to the proper belief. Let's look at what proper belief looks like. Here is how Merriam Webster defines belief:

"a state or habit of mind in which trust or confidence is placed in some person or thing."

Now here is what trust or confidence in GOD looks like:

⁴ By faith Abel offered unto God a more excellent sacrifice than Cain, by which he obtained witness that he was righteous, God testifying of his gifts: and by it he being dead yet speaketh. ⁵ By faith Enoch was translated that he should not see death; and was not found, because God had translated him: for before his translation he had this testimony, that he pleased God. ⁶ But without faith it is impossible to please him: for he that cometh to God must believe that he is, and that he is a rewarder of them that diligently seek him. ⁷ By faith Noah, being warned of God of things not seen as yet, moved with fear, prepared an ark to the saving of his house; by the which he condemned the world, and became heir of the righteousness which is by faith. ⁸ By faith Abraham, when he was called to go out into a place which he should after receive for an inheritance, obeyed; and he went out, not knowing whither he went. ⁹ By faith he sojourned in the land of promise, as in a strange country, dwelling in tabernacles with Isaac and Jacob, the heirs with him of the same promise: ¹⁰ For he looked for a city which hath foundations, whose builder and maker is God. ¹¹ Through faith also Sara herself received strength to conceive seed, and was delivered of a child when she was past age, because she judged him faithful who had promised. ¹² Therefore sprang there even of one, and him as good as dead, so many as the stars of the sky in multitude, and as the sand which is by the sea shore innumerable. ¹³ These all died in faith, not having received the promises, but having seen them afar off, and were persuaded of them, and embraced them, and confessed that they were strangers and pilgrims on the earth. ¹⁴ For they that say such things declare plainly that they seek a country. ¹⁵ And truly, if they had been mindful of that country from whence they came out, they might have had opportunity to have returned. ¹⁶ But now they desire a better country, that is, an heavenly: wherefore God is not ashamed to be called their God: for he hath prepared for them a city. (Hebrews 11:4-16 KJV)

Belief in GOD is reflected by obedience to Him.

⁶ Whosoever abideth in him sinneth not: whosoever sinneth hath not seen him, neither known him. ⁷ Little children, let no man deceive you: he that doeth righteousness is righteous, even as he is righteous. ⁸ He that committeth sin is of the devil; for the devil sinneth from the beginning. For this purpose the Son of God was manifested, that he might destroy the works of the devil. ⁹ Whosoever is born of God doth not commit sin; for his seed remaineth in him: and he cannot sin, because he is born of God. ¹⁰ In this the children of God are manifest, and the children of the devil: whosoever doeth not righteousness is not of God, neither he that loveth not his brother. (1 John 3:6-10 KJV)

We have the apostles writing all of these letters to the various members of the body of Christ so they could judge themselves, and also distinguish between those who had truly received the Gospel of Christ versus those who were still walking in the vanity of their own minds and disobedience. These letters were written by men who had no concept of the separation of church and state, nor the concept of going to the corner church on Sunday to be taught by pastor so and so or reverend doctor so and so. Christianity was central to their life, meaning their lives revolved around Christianity, not Christianity revolving around their lives. They were not trying to conform Christianity to their way of life; they were trying to conform their lives to the teachings of Christ.

They understood how integral their lives were and how that ethically called for accountability.

If what I do has an impact on you and your family, then I should be accountable to you for my actions. Today, that statement is a little hard to digest. Now let me make it a little harder. If *your* actions have impact on me and my family, then *you* should be accountable to me for *your* actions. Almost immediately, your freedom feels infringed upon. People have the false belief that when they become an adult, they are free to do whatever they want to do. No one escapes cause and effect, sowing and reaping. Free implies no one will have to pay. Every man will pay for his actions. Some will pay now, and some will pay later, but there is a reckoning for everyone. It is better to reckon with your actions now, while you can still repent, than to face judgment for them before GOD.

People live so isolated from one another until it becomes difficult to understand how our lives impact our neighbors. One of my spiritual mentors once said, "exchange is the process of life." If your isolation prevents you from exchanging what GOD has given you for others, then you are robbing them. See, it is what we do as well as what we don't do, which has an impact on those around us. Walking out the mandates of love can be daunting in our own strength and knowledge; that is exactly why GOD has made His Spirit and Word accessible to us. These letters were written by those conscious of the fact that the devil is a great deceiver, so to counter and defend against his tactics they were publishing truth and light. By shedding light on the topic of what belief looks like, people could be warned in the event they, or someone they knew, had been deceived into thinking they were in the Way, when they were actually lost.

The introduction of the gospel of Christ was totally new to the world. Though the coming of Christ and His new covenant had been prophesied through the Old Testament, it was still earthshaking. The freedom of the spirit requires the integrity of a dedicated heart. Anyone not born again will abuse the liberty represented in the New Testament for an opportunity to be even more carnal. Back then, as well as now, people try to justify living carnally with vain reasoning, thinking since Christ has fulfilled the law then they should be free from confinement and penalty of any regulations, and since Christ paid for all their sins, there is no need to do any accounting.

To believe the testimony of Christ, you must first know something about Him. If that which you know of Christ is true, and you believe it in your heart, it will bear fruit of righteousness. You will not be looking to circumnavigate it; you will be looking to implement it into your life and get more.

> *Again, the kingdom of heaven is like unto treasure hid in a field; the which when a man hath found, he hideth, and for joy thereof goeth and selleth all that he hath, and buyeth that field.* (Matthew 13:44 KJV)

So those doing the work of the gospel need to judge themselves to be sure they are in the Way and not deceptively serving some other influence, like their ego, a guilty conscience, or the flesh. The preaching of the gospel has to come from a pure heart, which is a heart surrendered to the truth in YESHUA HAMASHIACH. Take a look at this warning, which the Apostle Paul wrote to Timothy regarding those who teach false doctrines:

> *³ As I besought thee to abide still at Ephesus, when I went into Macedonia, that thou mightest charge some that they teach no other doctrine, ⁴ Neither give heed to fables and endless genealogies, which minister questions, rather than godly edifying which is in faith: so do. ⁵ Now the end of the commandment is charity out of a pure heart, and of a good conscience, and of faith unfeigned: ⁶ From which some having swerved have turned aside unto vain jangling; ⁷ Desiring to be teachers of the law; understanding neither what they say, nor whereof they affirm.* (1Timothy 1:3-7)

Paul is telling Timothy that the result of the commission is love out of a pure heart, and a good conscience, and faith without fiction. To get this result, the seed sown must be pure, based on the true testimony of Christ. It can't be a gospel based on men's traditions or a gospel conformed to what is compliant to current social standards. It must be the gospel of the eternal Word of GOD based on faith. This is the only seed that can produce the belief that saves and glorifies GOD.

CHAPTER 5
THE LIES AND THE DARKNESS

W hy would Eve believe the lie from the serpent, that death or destruction would not be a consequence of disobeying GOD? You may think that was foolish of her, but many people still believe that lie today. Many people believe that rebelling against GOD, will not result in destruction. As you read what I am saying about rebellion, your mind would suggest people outside of a church setting, but in actuality that would be the wrong group of people. Just like Adam and Eve, those who rebel against GOD are those who have been acquainted with Him. You can't disobey GOD until you first know what He has said.

> *Therefore to him that knoweth to do good, and doeth it not, to him it is sin.* (James 4:17 KJV)

The lost are just that, lost. It is the one who has been given direction yet chooses to detour that walks in rebellion and will get the harsher judgment. This is relevant because the serpent is still seducing people unto death by his lies. Just as Adam and Eve obviously didn't believe disobeying the command of GOD would lead to death and expulsion from the garden, many Christians today don't believe that their continuing to live carnally will lead to being rejected by GOD, and a forfeiture of a heavenly address. Here is what scripture says,

> *Know ye not that the unrighteous shall not inherit the kingdom of God? Be not deceived: neither fornicators, nor idolaters, nor adulterers, nor effeminate, nor abusers of themselves with mankind, Nor thieves, nor covetous, nor drunkards, nor revilers, nor extortioners, shall inherit the kingdom of God.* (1 Corinthians 6:9-10 KJV)

If you are guilty of any of these carnal acts and believe yourself to be a citizen of GOD's kingdom, then just as Adam and Eve, you have been deceived. My intent here is not to bring condemnation but rather clarification. Likewise, the intent of Roman 8 was not to imply a free pass to heaven for those who live carnally. Read it closely:

> *There is therefore now no condemnation to them which are in Christ Jesus, **who walk not after the flesh, but after the Spirit**.* (Romans 8:1 KJV)

What is my motive for sharing this? I don't want your money. I am not trying to control you or exploit you. I am sharing this to combat the darkness, which impacts all our lives. My heart also breaks for Christ as I think of all He has done to set us free and win our hearts, yet He still has to watch many of His people remain bound and oppressed because they feel He is asking for too much to save them. This distortion of values has kept people from accepting the cross of Christ, which is the path to new spiritual life.

I was asked recently to lead a men's Bible study, and as I searched the spirit of YAHWEH within me, I felt compelled to speak on sin and dis-unity in the church today. I have heard so many say in recent times, "Where is the impact of the followers of Christ today?" The real question is: Where is the body of Christ today? Where are those who walk in His image from being filled with His life? For us to see those raised with resurrection power and living righteously in His image, we must first have those who are willing to die in the likeness of His death. Before we can die in the likeness of His death, we need to understand what His death encompassed. The key aspect of His death that I want to focus on here is that He surrendered His life willingly. Christ died as a result of Him freely giving His life. No man took it. We know that YESHUA HAMASHIACH is GOD, and no one or anything could have taken His life anyway. He had to lay it down. Many people tend to focus on the brutality Christ faced on His way to Calvary as the costliest aspect of His death, but I believe the costliest aspect was the riches of His glory. If people could just perceive the splendor of YESHUA's glory in Heaven before His descent into the earth, I believe they wouldn't focus so much on what He suffered in the flesh. Not to say what He suffered in the earth wasn't momentous, but to understand more fully the majesty of who suffered it is a much bigger deal. Christ was GOD in the flesh. It took six words to state that, but it takes so much more to really apprehend that. YESHUA HAMASHIACH literally made everything … every star and planet you see, everything and everyone on the earth. He is before and above everything, and He left that preeminence so that you could know in His eyes it would mean even more if He could share it with you. Why else would He leave it all and humble Himself to the frailty of a body of flesh and allow *us* to put Him to death? I get the feeling that none of those nails or flesh-ripping weapons used on Him hurt as much as losing one of us. To Him, it was all worth it. Now the question is, how much is He worth to you?

We have the chance to show just how much every day when we awake to a new day. The Apostle Paul wrote in a letter that because of all YESHUA gave up to redeem us, the least we could do is give our lives to Him to do what He pleases. It is not just the reasonable thing to do; it is the right thing to do. For us to be seen in the earth, walking in the likeness of His glory, we need to die in the likeness of His death. We need to willfully surrender everything we are and everything we have to Him. That is the death of the cross. Once we do that, His life in us can manifest freely. He can form and fashion our lives for

His glory. We truly become His workmanship. People will see a manifestation of the body of Christ.

Now many people have confessed "The sinner's prayer," but how many have actually chosen to die in the likeness of Christ? How many have chosen to give up everything unto pain of death to lay hold on His life? Lip service isn't new in the earth. In a letter to the Hebrew Christians, the author said that none of them had resisted unto blood, striving against sin. Sin is rampant among confessing Christians because they refuse to suffer in the flesh. The cross we have been called to bear is painful to the flesh. We need to come to terms with that up front. Peter wrote in his letter to the Thessalonians that the one who has learned to suffer in the flesh has ceased from sin (1 Peter 4:1 KJV). Honestly, most of the sins that still entrap many confessing Christians today could be mastered if there were more of a willingness to suffer for righteousness than to please the flesh. Most of the sinful appetites we have will be extinguished as our souls are healed and our minds are renewed, but until that transformation happens, we simply have to resist and suffer for righteousness sake. If you truly know YESHUA, if you have had a revelation of Him and all that He has done for you, then the compelling of His love will give you the will and His spirit will give you the power to stand in resistance of evil. As Paul wrote in the letters to the church in Rome, sin will not have dominion over you.

Christ endured the cross, empowered by the vision on the other side of it. Before He was nailed to the cross, He had already embraced it. He didn't go to the cross kicking and screaming. Right before He descended the furthest away from His former glory, He asked the Father, in the frailness of humanity, could He avoid having to go through what was before Him, and what it was that He had to endure. He had to deny Himself, just as He is asking us to do. Understand, GOD is faithful and true: He is the Light of the world, the proclaimer of Truth and reality, the reckoner of all evil, the Creator, Life itself, One who has always been, and He has to quietly accept our evil upon Him, condemnation, and death. After the cross, His testimony reads a lot different:

I am he that liveth, and was dead; and, behold, I am alive for evermore, Amen; and have the keys of hell and of death. (Revelations 1:18 KJV)

If we will die in the likeness of His death, He will give us His keys to use. Amen! This is what the lies and darkness of the enemy are trying to keep us from. Ruling with Christ and subduing the earth in righteousness. Crushing the kingdom of darkness and delivering souls from the realm of darkness. We must renounce everything that does not align with the Truth of GOD—first, in our own lives, and then in the world around us. Before we can do this, we must first know Truth, the person. Christ proclaimed, *I am the Way, the Truth, and the Life...* (John 14:6 KJV)

And such as do wickedly against the covenant shall he corrupt by flatteries: but the people that do know their God shall be strong, and do exploits. (Daniel 11:32 KJV)

CHAPTER 6
ISRAEL OUR FORERUNNER

YAHWEH is sovereign. He even rules over time. He is the Alpha and the Omega, the beginning and the end. He moves in and out of time according to the counsel of His will. He shows us the end from the beginning to display that He is the author and finisher of fate, also to give us hope and to build our faith in Him. YAHWEH is a wonderful teacher and counselor. He utilizes examples and metaphors to help us see His will and understand the paths of life. Blessed are those He chooses to reveal His truth to. He is the source of light and according to the counsel of His will He causes light to shine in darkness. I testify according to His abundant mercy and grace; He has pierced the darkness of my soul by His Spirit, to cause me to see many things in the light of His truth. Things, which are irrefutable, such as what I am sharing here regarding our salvation.

YAHWEH has given this generation the lives of thousands of people over thousands of years as examples of what He is performing in this day, so that we might understand the Way, the Truth, and the Life. YESHUA HAMASHIACH, the savior of the world has been foretold all through scripture, from Genesis to Malachi. The most prolific example of the salvation before us is the journey and trials of the children of Israel. YAHWEH chose them to demonstrate the gospel of Christ thousands of years before His ministry. In His justice, they will receive great favor and mercy, for He is truly a good GOD. This generation must learn from the example set before us at such great cost.

> *Moreover, brethren, I do not want you to be unaware that all our fathers were under the cloud, all passed through the sea, ² all were baptized into Moses in the cloud and in the sea, ³ all ate the same spiritual food, ⁴ and all drank the same spiritual drink. For they drank of that spiritual Rock that followed them, and that Rock was Christ. ⁵ But with most of them God was not well pleased, for their bodies were scattered in the wilderness. ⁶ Now these things became our examples, to the intent that we should not lust after evil things as they also lusted. ⁷ And do not become idolaters as were some of them. As it is written, "The people sat down to eat and drink, and rose up to play." ⁸ Nor let us commit sexual immorality, as some of them did, and in one day twenty-three thousand fell; ⁹ nor let us tempt Christ, as some of them also tempted, and were destroyed by serpents; ¹⁰ nor complain, as some of them also complained, and were destroyed by the destroyer. ¹¹ Now all these things happened to them as examples, and they were written for our admonition, upon whom the ends of the ages have come.* (1 Corinthians 10:1-11 NKJV)

Through an examination of YAHWEH's deliverance of the children of Israel and their journey to the promise land, we can come to a better understanding of our journey through the salvation of YESHUA HAMASHIACH to our eternal inheritance. First, let us look at what Israel represents. Israel represents the bride ordained to enter a covenant relationship with GOD and to bring forth His holy seed. Israel was also a foretelling of the marriage between Christ and the church. Even before Israel, Adam and Eve in the garden were a foretelling of this holy marriage to come. In sticking with the example of Israel, GOD is holy and will only make covenant with a holy bride. Israel, after being captive in Egypt for four hundred years, had been defiled. She wasn't defiled by the dirt and slime of the brick pits; she was defiled by opening her heart to the pleasures and ways of Egypt. YAHWEH, being amazingly merciful, was still willing to accept her though she had been defiled. She only needed to turn her heart to her deliverer and allow Him to cleanse her. Even though GOD had separated His bride from Egypt, His bride would not separate Egypt from her heart. She kept comparing GOD to her sadistic Egyptian lover and as astonishing as it may be, her affections stayed with Egypt. Let's look at the record.

THE DEFEAT OF PHARAOH

We look at the Pharaoh of Egypt and think, he was totally delusional and mad, but YAHWEH hardened his heart to the point that he was as perverted in mind as Satan, who also challenged GOD. Through YAHWEH's battle with Pharaoh, He proved that all of Egypt's false gods were powerless with each plague. The last plague with which YAHWEH smote Egypt gave us the observance of Passover, which is a foretelling of the sacrifice of the Lamb of GOD, YESHUA HAMASHIACH. Any life covered with the blood of Christ is saved, just as all of those in Israel who had the blood of a lamb on their doorpost were spared. Pharaoh's final defeat came when his army and weapons of warfare were engulfed by the Red Sea. This is a foretelling of how Satan would be defeated by the life in the blood of YESHUA HAMASHIACH. For all those deceived and taken captive by the lies of Satan, there is deliverance through the propitiation in the blood of Christ. The blood of Christ erased all the sin of disobedience wrought by man as he lived alienated from the holy and righteous GOD through carnal filth. The blood spilled through the suffering of Christ didn't accuse mankind, as Satan had hoped; instead, the blood of Christ pleaded for our forgiveness, paid for our sins, and lifted the curses upon our lives. The blood of Christ appeased the wrath of YAHWEH and restored our divine kinship.

> *And you, being dead in your trespasses and the uncircumcision of your flesh, He has made alive together with Him, having forgiven you all trespasses, ¹⁴ having wiped out the handwriting of requirements that was against us, which was contrary to us. And He has taken it out of the way, having nailed it to the cross. ¹⁵ Having disarmed principalities and powers, He made a public spectacle of them, triumphing over them in it.*
> (Colossians 2:13-15 NKJV)

The blood of Christ, being the life of an obedient son, gave all those who accepted His blood the power to become obedient sons. To accept this new life, you have to be willing to part with your old life. This brings us to Israel's journey through the wilderness.

Even after the power of Pharaoh had been destroyed, Israel had to be cleansed from the rudiments of Egypt's perversion to become a fitting bride for GOD. The passage through the desert to Mt. Sinai was designed for that purpose. This is the New Testament equivalent of the bride of Christ taking up the cross. Let's juxtapose the New Testament salvation journey on what we have covered so far. Christ has defeated Satan by breaking the power of sin, delivering us from fear, and giving us a way out of bondage. In giving us the light of truth and revealing His everlasting love, we are free to seek and fulfill our true purpose for living: a fruitful covenant relationship with GOD. Passing through the Red Sea is accepting the deliverance, but this does not complete our salvation; it brings us to the cross where the transformation, which is needed for receiving the fullness of it, can begin.

YAHWEH uses the wilderness as a place to begin the transformation of Israel. It is a place of mortifying the flesh in preparation for walking with a spiritual GOD. It is a place of fasting and learning to rely on GOD. If properly embraced, the wilderness would have prepared Israel to receive the laws of GOD. Instead, Israel resented the wilderness and would not submit their thoughts and imaginations to the obedience of GOD. This is where Israel earned the name of being a "stiff necked" people, because they would not bow their heads to GOD. Israel in their ungratefulness provoked GOD to wrath. In His wrath, GOD proclaimed that no one who had come from Egypt would enter the Promised Land; instead He would only admit the children born in the wilderness who had not been defiled by Egypt. This is an example of the cross of Christ. YESHUA proclaimed that if anyone wanted to follow Him, they would need to take up their cross and deny themselves. He also taught that a person had to be born again in order to enter the Kingdom of GOD. Israel demonstrated that the carnal man cannot inherit the promise of GOD therefore, the carnal life must be put to death in order for the spiritual life to be manifested unto obtaining the promise.

The promise of salvation brings forward the same requirements as the requirements for entering the Promised Land. This is YAHWEH's way of giving us an example beforehand so that we could better understand how to receive the salvation of Christ. We must be willing to release our former lives with their habits and proclivities in order to inherit the promise of a new and better life. We must have a grateful heart in pursuing GOD for the great work of deliverance needed to set us free to truly live. We have to be willing to live from His dictionary of terms and follow His maps for life and accept His codes of conduct. We must be willing to start our lives over by accepting His spiritual reset. If this seems like a big ask, it is only because your affections have not yet shifted to the things of GOD, and you haven't fully comprehended your need for salvation. It also means you have not gotten a spiritual glimpse of the life on the other side of the cross. The carnal eye can only see the cross, with the pain and anguish of its nails and the open display of shame. By accepting the nails in your hands and feet, you agree to being painfully restricted to any acts of the flesh. It is the end of crafting carnal things through the works of your hands, and the end of walking the paths to carnal destinations. The cross reveals to all your worldly lovers, friends, and associates that you have rejected everything they value, and it has left you naked and without anything in the world. I must say that few Christians have accepted the shame of the cross because they still labor to be rich, to preserve their own reputation, and to save face, but Christ truly humbled Himself and surrendered all. It is written,

> *Looking unto Jesus the author and finisher of our faith; who for the joy that was set before him endured the cross, despising the shame, and is set down at the right hand of the throne of God.* (Hebrews 12:2 KJV)

If we will rise in the likeness of His glory, we must be willing to humble ourselves in the likeness of His death. It is written:

> *⁴ Therefore we are buried with him by baptism into death: that like as Christ was raised up from the dead by the glory of the Father, even so we also should walk in newness of life. ⁵ For if we have been planted together in the likeness of his death, we shall be also in the likeness of his*

resurrection: ⁶ Knowing this, that our old man is crucified with him, that the body of sin might be destroyed, that henceforth we should not serve sin. (Romans 6:4-6 KJV)

Egypt was a great empire as the values of the world go. The Israelites married into the Egyptian culture and identified with its glory despite the wickedness. Due to the unenlightened values of the Israelites, they found living in the shadow of Egypt more glorious than living in the shadow of the Almighty. The tents and manna of the wilderness just didn't measure up to the buildings and fleshpots of Egypt. Their spiritual dullness would not allow them to value the liberty and glory of GOD they had been blessed with higher than their oppressive lifestyle in Egypt.

THE WILDERNESS AND MOUNT SINAI

Can we hang on the cross until the Life of GOD comes? The first destination planned for the children of Israel was mount Sinai. It was there that YAHWEH planned to give them the means to abide in His presence.

> *"1 In the third month, when the children of Israel were gone forth out of the land of Egypt, the same day came they into the wilderness of Sinai. 2 For they were departed from Rephidim, and were come to the desert of Sinai, and had pitched in the wilderness; and there Israel camped before the mount. 3 And Moses went up unto God, and the Lord called unto him out of the mountain, saying, Thus shalt thou say to the house of Jacob, and tell the children of Israel; 4 Ye have seen what I did unto the Egyptians, and how I bare you on eagles' wings, and brought you unto myself. 5 Now therefore, if ye will obey my voice indeed, and keep my covenant, then ye shall be a peculiar treasure unto me above all people: for all the earth is mine: 6 And ye shall be unto me a kingdom of priests, and an holy nation. These are the words which thou shalt speak unto the children of Israel. 7 And Moses came and called for the elders of the people, and laid before their faces all these words which the Lord commanded him.* (Exodus 19:1-7 KJV)

Once the children of Israel arrived at Mt. Sinai, Moses would ascend the mountain and bring back the means to translate them into a holy people, the laws and ordinances of GOD. The laws and ordinances symbolize the mind and heart of GOD. Unfortunately, the children of Israel would not confine themselves to the wilderness; they ventured back to Egypt in recalling the ways of the Egyptians and created a false god while waiting for the manifestation of the gift He promised. This example is given to us so that we can patiently wait in the humility of the cross and in the hope of the promise, not looking back to our former life, and be in position to receive the gift of GOD: the gift of GOD being the life of Christ through the power of the Holy Spirit.

The life of Christ transforms us into exactly what YAHWEH told Moses He had planned for the children of Israel.

> *⁷ Unto you therefore which believe he is precious: but unto them which be disobedient, the stone which the builders disallowed, the same is made the head of the corner, ⁸ And a stone of stumbling, and a rock of offence, even to them which stumble at the word, being disobedient: whereunto also they were appointed. ⁹ But ye are a chosen generation, a royal priesthood, an holy nation, a peculiar people; that ye should shew forth the praises of him who hath called you out of darkness into his marvellous light; ¹⁰ Which in time past were not a people, but are now the people of God: which had not obtained mercy, but now have obtained mercy.* (1 Peter 2:7-10 KJV)

YAHWEH has called us out of the world to the holy mount of His presence, to receive the gift of our inheritance brought down to us by YESHUA HAMASHIACH, Jesus the Messiah. We must continue to mortify the flesh on the cross, that the life of Christ might be revealed in us. We must persevere until we lay hold on the life of the spirit and the mind of Christ, so that we can have fellowship with GOD, and truly be His people, in His likeness, holy and righteous.

CHAPTER 7
WWJD

For many years now, there has been this popular concept regarding the best way for Christians to make life decisions. The concept involved simply asking yourself, "What Would Jesus Do?" and then following that line as best you could. Someone gave me a bracelet with the acronym "WWJD" as a reminder to utilize this concept. I wore it on a few occasions and then got a check in my spirit on the whole concept. I realized that it was just another piece of fruit cast from the tree of the knowledge of good and evil. The "WWJD" concept compels men to draw from their intellect and reasoning, instead of faith and the spirit. Knowing the mind and will of GOD is dependent on the person being born again in Christ and having the power of the Holy Spirit come into the heart and mind as a light shining in darkness. This makes it possible to apprehend the things of GOD. Some people believe it is impossible to understand GOD, but that is only true for those not born again.

⁹ But as it is written, Eye hath not seen, nor ear heard, neither have entered into the heart of man, the things which God hath prepared for them that love him. ¹⁰ But God hath revealed them unto us by his Spirit: for the Spirit searcheth all things, yea, the deep things of God. ¹¹ For what man

> *knoweth the things of a man, save the spirit of man which is in him? even so the things of God knoweth no man, but the Spirit of God. ¹² Now we have received, not the spirit of the world, but the spirit, which is of God; that we might know the things that are freely given to us of God. ¹³ Which things also we speak, not in the words which man's wisdom teacheth, but which the Holy Ghost teacheth; comparing spiritual things with spiritual.* (1 Cor 2:9-13 KJV)

All revelation of truth comes from the spirit of GOD. The only way to live in the truth of GOD is to have the truth of GOD live in you. This happens through the resurrection power of the spirit of GOD through YESHUA HAMASHIACH.

> *¹¹ He came unto his own, and his own received him not. ¹² But as many as received him, to them gave he power to become the sons of God, even to them that believe on his name: ¹³ Which were born, not of blood, nor of the will of the flesh, nor of the will of man, but of God.* (John 1:11-13 KJV)

To know What Jesus Would Do, you must become what Jesus was, a son born of GOD. The only way to become a son of GOD is through the seed of Christ. You must receive Christ into your heart with belief for this transformation to occur. I am writing this so that all may understand that this is not something that can occur simply from graduating from seminary, or going to church frequently, or living in a monastery, or any other efforts of man. This new birth comes from surrendering the possibility to faith in GOD's ability—hence, the cross. Surely you will grow through exposure to the word of GOD and the ministry of the church, but it is foundational to understand the transformation comes from GOD's power and not your own. Even the knowledge of GOD is His gift without your own merit.

> *¹⁶ Cease not to give thanks for you, making mention of you in my prayers; ¹⁷ That the God of our Lord Jesus Christ, the Father of glory, may give*

unto you the spirit of wisdom and revelation in the knowledge of him: ¹⁸ *The eyes of your understanding being enlightened; that ye may know what is the hope of his calling, and what the riches of the glory of his inheritance in the saints,* ¹⁹ *And what is the exceeding greatness of his power to us-ward who believe, according to the working of his mighty power,* ²⁰ *Which he wrought in Christ, when he raised him from the dead, and set him at his own right hand in the heavenly places,* ²¹ *Far above all principality, and power, and might, and dominion, and every name that is named, not only in this world, but also in that which is to come:* ²² *And hath put all things under his feet, and gave him to be the head over all things to the church,* ²³ *Which is his body, the fulness of him that filleth all in all.* (Ephesians 1:16-23 KJV)

Also,

⁸ *For by grace are ye saved through faith; and that not of yourselves: it is the gift of God:* ⁹ *Not of works, lest any man should boast.* ¹⁰ *For we are his workmanship, created in Christ Jesus unto good works, which God hath before ordained that we should walk in them.* (Ephesians 2:8-10 KJV)

These two blocks of scripture just cited from Ephesians explain what I have been writing about here. It is this rebirth into one spirit, the spirit of Christ, which gives the church true unity. I have had quite a few discussions over the years where another believer and I were debating the viewpoint of GOD on a particular topic. In some instances, it may be difficult for two believers to come to a consensus on GOD's viewpoint, but it should be rare given the aid of the Bible and the revelations of GOD's spirit. So then, what makes the task of unifying on the mind of GOD so difficult today? Here are the issues that I see:

1. The biggest issue today is that the church is so carnal.

But the natural man receiveth not the things of the Spirit of God: for they are foolishness unto him: neither can he know them, because they are spiritually discerned. (1 Corinthians 2:14 KJV)

People are often not on the same page with GOD because they are still dominated by inbred feelings and desires. Strong feelings do not equal truth. GOD didn't send His Son to suffer, die, and be resurrected for you to feel good about yourself. He sent His son to open your eyes to your true self, which lives in the spirit.

2. False teaching. So many people are taught that love is unconditional, and without judgment. However, from the Old Testament throughout the New Testament, the Bible is full of the "if" and "then" conditions surrounding fellowship with GOD and His blessings. I will give a couple of examples from YESHUA, since His meekness is so often confused with Him not having strong stands on what He will accept and reject.

    If ye keep my commandments, ye shall abide in my love; even as I have kept my Father's commandments, and abide in his love. (John 15:10 KJV)

    Ye are my friends, if ye do whatsoever I command you. (John 15:14 KJV)

    Judge not according to the appearance, but judge righteous judgment. (John 7: 24 KJV)

    23 But the hour cometh, and now is, when the true worshippers shall worship the Father in spirit and in truth: for the Father seeketh such to worship him. 24 God is a Spirit: and they that worship him must worship him in spirit and in truth. (John 4: 23-24 KJV)

GOD has come and established a standard, which He will not compromise for anyone because He can't deny Himself. That would be the doom of all creation. He is the way to life. We must conform to His standards because He alone is Life. In Matthew 7:14, when YESHUA states that narrow is the way and straight is the gate that leads to eternal life, and few there are that find it, it speaks to the point that there is no compromising the mandates of life. Life does not bend to us; we must bend to life. In order to walk the path of life, we must be willing to lay aside our preferences to stay on the path. Those unwilling to take up the cross will detour and be lost in their own way. By denying our carnal and worldly impulses, we give liberty to the spirit to reign in us and lead us in the way of Life. This is the circumcision of the flesh that enables us to be identified as children of GOD. The cross is the tool we use to perform this circumcision.

As the old man perishes, the new man created by the power of Christ in us grows stronger each day. As the new man flourishes, we grow in our knowledge of GOD's will and in our ability to walk in obedience to His word. We are relieved of the task of trying to figure out what Jesus would do by allowing the spirit to transform us into His likeness, in word and in deed.

CHAPTER 8
EMBRACING THE CROSS

The fact that salvation is a work of GOD's grace means that salvation has come to us without us having to qualify for it. It is like Christ winning the gold medal in the Olympics of life, and then telling you that you can stand on the podium with Him and be crowned a winner, but only if you will accept that He is the only way that you can become a winner, and you agree to let Him transform you. Then He tells you that in order to begin the process, you must first get off the couch and pick up the cross.

When this offer comes to you, you are 180 pounds overweight with high blood pressure, diabetes, bad knees, and congestive heart failure. His offer is that if you will believe in His power to change you and agree to pick up your cross every day, He will give you His perfect health in exchange for your body of death. The grace of GOD brings this offering to you based on His unmerited favor and concern for you, not because you stood out in any way. His love for you alone made you significant, and that never changes. No matter how fit you get, He will never love you more than He did when He found you on the couch, 180 pounds overweight. You must genuinely believe the testimony that He has already carried your 180 pounds and died from it, and afterwards was raised from the dead with the body of a champion and received the gold medal of life. Your belief in this testimony gives you the confidence to get up off the couch and commit to taking up your cross daily. In this example, taking up the cross is equivalent to getting off the couch and canceling all your media subscriptions, turning off the TV, as well as giving up all junk food. It is important to understand that none of this process is mere magic; it is actuality. Christ is transforming you into a champion who can compete just as He competed. He begins this process by removing your failing heart and giving you the heart of a champion. This is how you're able to walk the path of a champion and shed all that extra weight, which is killing you. It doesn't happen all at once, but every day you are transformed. On some days you lose ounces and on some days you shed pounds, but on every day you take up your cross, you are transformed.

Today, many confessing Christians don't rightly discern the proposition of salvation. They believe you are rewarded the Champion's crown without ever truly becoming a champion. They fail to realize you will actually have to run a race. Through the discipline of the Spirit, you will have to shed the extra weight and become a conditioned champion. We just have to commit to the journey and be willing to take at least one step every day. Our GOD is wonderful and can translate one step into a trip to heaven. When Christ appears, we are going to look like Him. As believers, we are being changed into His likeness every day. We are putting on His patience, His kindness, His obedience, His faithfulness, His righteousness, His peace, His temperance, His humility, and so on. Through the exchange life experience of the cross, we are exchanging the life of the old man of the earth with the life of the new man that is divine after Heaven. We are laying down our earthly nature in order to inherit Christ's divine nature. The result is that we are no longer ruled by sin unto death but are now free to serve righteousness unto life.

If we don't rightly discern this, we will still be sitting on the couch when Christ returns— looking at the TV with the 180 pounds of death binding us. What is worse, when we go to meet Him, thinking we are His chosen, He will not recognize us because we don't resemble Him. This is a metaphorical example of those who accept the offering of salvation but fail to meet the criteria of taking up their cross and making themselves ready. I know this is contrary to what many of you have been taught. Many confessing Christians are taught that Christ did "it" all on the cross, but the "it" is misrepresented. What Christ did for us completely was destroy every barrier and obstacle between the Father and us; this is putting the tree of Life again within our reach. He has secured a place for us at the table of YAHWEH, but in order to take our seat there, we first must push away from the table of Satan. Since I know the belief purporting that we have nothing to do to be saved is such a stronghold, I am going to just let the Word of GOD speak for a moment:

Then said Jesus unto his disciples, If any man will come after me, let him deny himself, and take up his cross, and follow me. (Matt 16:24 KJV) This quote of YESHUA is captured in the books of Mark and Luke as well.

34 And take heed to yourselves, lest at any time your hearts be overcharged with surfeiting, and drunkenness, and cares of this life, and so that day come upon you unawares. 35 For as a snare shall it come on all them that dwell on the face of the whole earth. 36 Watch ye therefore, and pray always, that ye may be accounted worthy to escape all these things that shall come to pass, and to stand before the Son of man. (Luke 21:34-36 KJV)

In the whole chapter of Matthew 25, YESHUA gave three different parables, each had the same message. I will share one parable:

"31 When the Son of man shall come in his glory, and all the holy angels with him, then shall he sit upon the throne of his glory: 32 And before him shall be gathered all nations: and he shall separate them one from another, as a shepherd divideth his sheep from the goats: 33 And he shall set the sheep on his right hand, but the goats on the left. 34 Then shall the King say unto them on his right hand, Come, ye blessed of my Father, inherit the kingdom prepared for you from the foundation of the world: 35 For I was an hungred, and ye gave me meat: I was thirsty, and ye gave me drink: I was a stranger, and ye took me in: 36 Naked, and ye clothed

me: I was sick, and ye visited me: I was in prison, and ye came unto me.
37 Then shall the righteous answer him, saying, Lord, when saw we thee
an hungred, and fed thee? or thirsty, and gave thee drink? 38 When saw
we thee a stranger, and took thee in? or naked, and clothed thee? 39 Or
when saw we thee sick, or in prison, and came unto thee? 40 And the King
shall answer and say unto them, Verily I say unto you, Inasmuch as ye
have done it unto one of the least of these my brethren, ye have done it
unto me. 41 Then shall he say also unto them on the left hand, Depart
from me, ye cursed, into everlasting fire, prepared for the devil and his
angels: 42 For I was an hungred, and ye gave me no meat: I was thirsty,
and ye gave me no drink: 43 I was a stranger, and ye took me not in:
naked, and ye clothed me not: sick, and in prison, and ye visited me not.
44 Then shall they also answer him, saying, Lord, when saw we thee an
hungred, or athirst, or a stranger, or naked, or sick, or in prison, and did
not minister unto thee? 45 Then shall he answer them, saying, Verily I say
unto you, Inasmuch as ye did it not to one of the least of these, ye did it
not to me. 46 And these shall go away into everlasting punishment: but the
righteous into life eternal." (Matt 25:31-46 KJV)

15 Beware of false prophets, which come to you in sheep's clothing, but in-
wardly they are ravening wolves. 16 Ye shall know them by their fruits. Do
men gather grapes of thorns, or figs of thistles? 17 Even so every good tree
bringeth forth good fruit; but a corrupt tree bringeth forth evil fruit. 18 A
good tree cannot bring forth evil fruit, neither can a corrupt tree bring
forth good fruit. 19 Every tree that bringeth not forth good fruit is hewn
down, and cast into the fire. 20 Wherefore by their fruits ye shall know
them. 21 Not every one that saith unto me, Lord, Lord, shall enter into the
kingdom of heaven; but he that doeth the will of my Father which is in
heaven. (Matt 7:15-21 KJV)

Those are examples from the very mouth of YESHUA Himself. These verses aren't to make you feel as if you must earn anything. It is just to show
you the fruit produced by those who truly believe the testimony of Christ

and know Him. If you truly love Him, then you will forsake your own way and follow Him, and He will lead you in the way everlasting. Do not allow yourself to be burdened by the need to bear fruit. Just focus on getting to know the planter. When was the last time you saw an apple tree sweat or strain? Root yourself in His word and continue to stretch for the light of truth, and you will be fruitful.

I am the vine, ye are the branches: He that abideth in me, and I in him, the same bringeth forth much fruit: for without me ye can do nothing. (John 15:5 KJV)

The key is getting into His word so that His word can get into you; then you will be fruitful. Seek the word of GOD as an expression of His heart and mind, with the intent of getting to know and understand Him, because He is truly beautiful. Your fruit will appear bountifully and organically.

CHAPTER 9
FORNICATION

The Lord is calling His body into unity. He is not calling us into mere agreement; He is calling us into spiritual unity. If we will be one, it will come from surrendering to the rule of His spirit. The biggest hindrance to our unity is carnality and pride. If we will not mortify our flesh and humble ourselves, we will not be able to fulfill the mandates of spiritual unity, and even worse, we will not be able to commune with the spirit of GOD to inherit the abundant life which abides in His presence.

As I write this, there is another call for unity coming from the world. As this society tries to recover from worldwide protesting in response to the continuation of institutional racism, there is an escalated call for tolerance toward the goal of unity. This call for unity by the world is carnal in nature and excludes the sovereignty of GOD. It is like the unity of the post flood generation, which began building the Tower of Babel. Their unity was centered on their own imagination and desires instead of GOD. GOD knew that this would lead to a reprobate society, so He divided them by breaking their communication. I saw a commercial recently, and it was set to music, with the voice of a charismatic orator rallying people together around the need for more love and tolerance, and for a better living for all people, with images of people representing their various life styles, including those life styles which GOD forbids. It was very seductive in its pitch for unity without the sovereign GOD, but I recognized it as another call to build the Tower of Babel. I am certain there were many confessing Christians who bit the bait through the carnality of their worldly affections. This is not the unity which we are being called to. Another name for ungodly union is fornication. Look at Revelations 2:14-23:

> *14 But I have a few things against thee, because thou hast there them that hold the doctrine of Balaam, who taught Balac to cast a stumbling block before the children of Israel, to eat things sacrificed unto idols, and to commit fornication. 15 So hast thou also them that hold the doctrine of the Nicolaitanes, which thing I hate. 16 Repent; or else I will come unto thee quickly, and will fight against them with the sword of my mouth. 17 He that hath an ear, let him hear what the Spirit saith unto the churches; To him that overcometh will I give to eat of the hidden manna, and will give him a white stone, and in the stone a new name written, which no man knoweth saving he that receiveth it. 18 And unto the angel of the church in Thyatira write; These things saith the Son of God, who hath his eyes like unto a flame of fire, and his feet are like fine brass; 19 I know thy works, and charity, and service, and faith, and thy patience, and thy works; and the last to be more than the first. 20 Notwithstanding I have a few things against thee, because thou sufferest that woman Jezebel, which calleth herself a prophetess, to teach and to seduce my servants to commit fornication, and to eat things sacrificed unto idols. 21 And I gave her space to repent of her fornication; and she repented not. 22 Behold, I will cast her into a bed, and them that commit adultery with her into great tribulation, except they repent of their deeds. 23 And I will kill her children with death; and all the churches shall know that I am he which searcheth the reins and hearts: and I will give unto every one of you according to your works."* (Revelations 2:14-23 KJV)

The Lord requires our total allegiance, and it is not for His benefit but for ours. This gets back to the fear of the Lord. When you understand that He alone is life and that His will is the sustenance of our life, then we start to see the futility in trying to accomplish anything lasting without Him. I have seen people struggle in marriages and relationships, trying to love based out of their feelings and emotions, instead of His spirit. As a result, they may stay together through agreements, but they never experience true unity. The difference between these two is like learning to tolerate another person playing their instrument versus learning to make lovely music together. GOD truly wants the best for us, which is why He has continually offered us Himself. I caution you from wasting your precious time on any endeavor not centered in Him. We experience spiritual unity when YAHWEH becomes our treasure, and our lives are spent in pursuit of Him.

We are warned in the book of Ephesians, chapter 5, not to be fornicators or whoremongers. At the core of each of these evils is giving ourselves for something other than the pleasure of GOD. When I say giving ourselves, I am referring to how we spend our lives. You will be filled with what you spend your life on. What we control of our lives is how we spend our time, our focus, and our efforts. If we spend our lives on GOD, we will be rewarded abundantly with eternal treasures, which will never perish. Here is the promise of GOD, *"The blessing of the Lord, it maketh rich, and he addeth no sorrow with it."* (Proverbs 10:22 KJV) If we spend our lives on carnal things, which will perish, then we will also perish being filled with them. The result of ungodly union is death; therefore, we need to be faithful brides unto the Lord.

CHAPTER 10
BECOMING A FAITHFUL BRIDE

The life of Christ is the gift almost too impossible to receive. Who will believe His report? Who will accept that all things are possible with GOD? Who will humble themselves to realize that their knowledge of GOD is not sufficient to doubt His capabilities against the record of Holy Scripture?

> *"Jesus said unto him, If thou canst believe, all things are possible to him that believeth."* (Mark 9:23 KJV)

Give GOD the freedom to be as big as He needs to be in your life by freeing Him from the parameters of your limited knowledge from which you draw your reasoning. There should be enough examples of things visible, which you can't explain, to credit the Creator with abilities and potential beyond the scope of your reasoning. The gift of the life of Christ abiding inside us to transform us into His divine likeness seems to wonderful to be real, but it is just what the Lord has done. The book of Ephesians does a great job of explaining the inner workings of this gift almost to wonderful to receive.

"⁴ But God, who is rich in mercy, for his great love wherewith he loved us, ⁵ Even when we were dead in sins, hath quickened us together with Christ, (by grace ye are saved;) ⁶ And hath raised us up together, and made us sit together in heavenly places in Christ Jesus: ⁷ That in the ages to come he might shew the exceeding riches of his grace in his kindness toward us through Christ Jesus." (Ephesians 2:4-7 KJV)

"Quickened" in this block of scripture comes from a combination of Greek words which means "to reanimate conjointly". The word "conjoin" means to join for a common purpose, like in marriage. So "quickened together with Christ" can be understood to mean "made alive again through marriage with Christ." Beautiful! The vows for this gracious and miraculous marriage take place at the altar of the cross. We give ourselves to be married with Christ at the cross. We must determine in our hearts to be faithful brides unto the Lord.

"They say, 'If a man divorces his wife, And she goes from him And becomes another man's, May he return to her again?' Would not that land be greatly polluted? But you have played the harlot with many lovers; Yet return to Me," says the LORD." (Jeremiah 3:1 NKJV)

Many confessing Christians have looked at the children of Israel and thought they had to be some of the most stubborn people who have walked the planet; however, we must remember that their hearts were veiled in sin and carnality. The anointing that was needed to interact with YAHWEH was shared very selectively. There were some major barriers between GOD and man. Today, that is not the case. We live in the days prophesied by the prophet Joel, when the Lord would pour out His spirit upon all flesh. The sacrifice of YESHUA destroyed the barrier between GOD and man.

¹² Seeing then that we have such hope, we use great plainness of speech: ¹³ And not as Moses, which put a veil over his face, that the children of Israel could not stedfastly look to the end of that which is abolished: ¹⁴ But their minds were blinded: for until this day remaineth the same vail untaken away in the reading of the old testament; which vail is done away in Christ. [15] But even unto this day, when Moses is read, the vail is upon their heart. [16] Nevertheless when it shall turn to the Lord, the vail shall be taken away. (2 Corinthians 3:12-16 KJV)

The love of GOD, through the face of YESHUA HAMASHIACH, has shined forth in a way like never before, parting the vail which covered the heart. If those called to be a bride of Christ aren't convinced of His love after the ministry of the cross and the gifts of the spirit, then I don't know what will persuade them. At the current moment, there are many confessing Christians still more enamored with this world and its pleasures than Christ and His kingdom of true love.

"And this is the condemnation, that light is come into the world, and men loved darkness rather than light, because their deeds were evil." (John 3:19 KJV)

Men have been deceived by the pleasures of darkness, not realizing that the cost is much greater than the temporal experiences. Christ has come in the light, disclosing up front, the cost of everlasting joy and peace with Him. A short time of suffering now for eternal bliss: however, many have chosen foolishly to have temporal pleasure now and eternal suffering later. Like so many stories and fables we have read, where people are lured off to their doom by a small measure of something satisfying with the promise of more to come, only to realize they have been lured into a trap, having left the true riches behind. This is the con of the wicked one. I see it all around me. I see people paying humongous costs for cheap thrills, which never satisfy. As true of all cheap things, they are abundant and easily obtained, so people become in bondage through the act of consumption, trying to sustain the fleeting satisfaction.

If they were willing to suffer for a season, in resisting temporal carnal pleasures, to get a true taste of life in the Spirit of Christ, they would realize the depth of the deception, which had them imprisoned. We cannot be fair weather friends of Christ. If you go at anything half-hearted, the results will be undesirable. We have to be committed lovers, forsaking all others. The church has to get rid of the adulteress heart. The Bible teaches that if the heart be single, then the whole body will be filled with light. The church will not reach its full glory until all of her affections shift from the world to the throne of YAHWEH. There are too many confessing Christians who are still attached and enamored with this world system. These are most often the people who have profited from the oppressive and murderous ways of this current world system, or those who hold misplaced hope that this world will turn from its current course. The wine of Babylon's fornication, spoken of in the book of Revelations, has dulled the senses of many confessing Christians. You can see it in their carnality and their cold love, which lacks empathy, humility, and compassion.

> *"And there followed another angel, saying, Babylon is fallen, is fallen, that great city, because she made all nations drink of the wine of the wrath of her fornication."* (Revelations 14:8 KJV)

They can't see that their lover is manipulating them through the gifts of carnal comfort, which blinds their spiritual eye. They profess their love for Christ from the bed of their fornication. The friend of the world is the enemy of GOD. You cannot serve two masters; you must hate one and love the other. Their uncleanness keeps them from truly knowing GOD, because they have not performed the preparation of a bride for holy marriage. It is time to repent and make yourselves ready while there is still time. How much time there is remaining is unknown.

> *33 Heaven and earth shall pass away: but my words shall not pass away. 34 And take heed to yourselves, lest at any time your hearts be overcharged with surfeiting, and drunkenness, and cares of this life, and so that day come upon you unawares. 35 For as a snare shall it come on all them that dwell on the face of the whole earth. 36 Watch ye therefore, and pray always, that ye may be accounted worthy to escape all these things that shall come to pass, and to stand before the Son of man.* (Luke 21:33-36 KJV)

For snares to work effectively they must be hidden, and when triggered, they must capture quickly and securely. Those who watch in the spirit cannot expect the world, which is blinded by carnality, to act in a sense of urgency these days. They are blind to the times and seasons of a spiritual GOD. Let's not be like the foolish virgins in Christ's parable of failing to stay prepared for His return.

> 25 *"1Then shall the kingdom of heaven be likened unto ten virgins, which took their lamps, and went forth to meet the bridegroom.*
>
> *2 And five of them were wise, and five were foolish. 3 They that were foolish took their lamps, and took no oil with them: 4 But the wise took oil in their vessels with their lamps. 5 While the bridegroom tarried, they all slumbered and slept. 6 And at midnight there was a cry made, Behold, the bridegroom cometh; go ye out to meet him. 7 Then all those virgins arose and trimmed their lamps. 8 And the foolish said unto the wise, Give us of your oil; for our lamps are gone out. 9 But the wise answered, saying, Not so; lest there be not enough for us and you: but go ye rather to them that sell, and buy for yourselves. 10 And while they went to buy, the bridegroom came; and they that were ready went in with him to the marriage: and the door was shut. 11 Afterward came also the other virgins, saying, Lord, Lord, open to us. 12 But he answered and said, Verily I say unto you, I know you not. 13 Watch therefore, for ye know neither the day nor the hour wherein the Son of man cometh." (Matthew 25:1-13 KJV)*

CHAPTER 11
GUARDING YOUR HEART

How do those who confess to love Christ end up in an adulteress relationship? Just like in the garden of Eden, the serpent tries to seduce us away from the one true Lover in all of history, into a destructive affair. We cannot allow the serpent, or this world, to define for us what love looks like. We cannot let our hearts get hard because GOD judges evil and corrects us. Where does your definition and perspective of love come from? Many followers of Christ will confess that He is the face of Love, but then experience dissonance as He speaks of casting the disobedient into outer darkness where there will be weeping and gnashing of teeth. Men will acknowledge GOD's right to judge as part of His sovereign power, but not necessarily as an attribute of His love. GOD's judgment is a direct attribute of His love and who He is. He is righteousness, and He has a day of reckoning for every element that opposes Him.

People see evil in the world and tend to fault GOD for it. Evil is the fruit of the abuse of freedom, granted by a loving GOD. Even though GOD has all power, He put earth under the authority of His children. The wicked one would be extremely limited in manifesting evil without man acting as the portal. Guard your heart from accepting accusations against GOD. We must look to one another for the accountability of evil. GOD is light, and the darkness corroding this world is a direct result of men rejecting the truth He illuminates. Those who reject GOD choose their fate. YAHWEH is the Alpha and the Omega, the beginning and the end. He is the conclusion that none of us will escape. Any Christian that co-signs on a solution to this world's problems, which fails to acknowledge the sovereignty of GOD, is compromised. It will not be well with anyone who refuses to submit to GOD. He has said through the prophet Isaiah, *"There is no peace, saith the Lord, unto the wicked."* (Isaiah 48:22 KJV) Who are the wicked? Those who refuse to submit themselves to the one who is love, righteousness, and life. New Testament followers of Christ must reconcile Him with the fiery acts of the Old Testament. There is but one GOD and His wrath will be unleashed again. This is why the letters of the New Testament exhort us to warn the wicked.

Many of those who confess to follow Christ have been seduced into loving soulishly instead of spiritually. What I mean by soulishly is filtering the love of GOD through earthly feelings and worldly reasoning. Christ shared with the disciples that He would have to be put to death, and upon hearing this Peter rebuked Christ. Peter's reaction is an example of soulish love. Peter responded from a place centered more on how it made him feel rather than what was actually necessary. Christ said that Peter didn't *savor* the things, which be of GOD. The word "savor" was translated from the Greek word *phroneo*, which means unable to "apprehend" or "have correct sentiments." At the time, Peter's affections were still seated in the realm of the carnal. Christ never changed His mission or His message based on the affections of those He ministered to. As the Author of life, He understands fully what is needed to save souls. Many of those trying to serve Christ present the gospel through a method of bait and switch. They are fishing for men with bait and a hook, instead of casting the net of the gospel.

5 Then Jesus saith unto them, Children, have ye any meat? They answered him, No.

⁶ And he said unto them, Cast the net on the right side of the ship, and ye shall find. They cast therefore, and now they were not able to draw it for the multitude of fishes. (John 21:5-6 KJV)

We must trust GOD with what goes on in the depths of men's heart, just as those disciples casting the net had to trust Christ with what was going on in the depths of the ocean. YESHUA told people upfront: if you want to walk with me, you are going to have to deny yourself, which means suffering in the flesh. Love is honest and abides in the light. The Gospel of Christ is divisive. Accept that. Understand that the sword of His spirit divides between that which is sustainable and that which is destined to fail, between that which tends to life and that which is sure to bring death. There is no liberty without the ability to choose. All those who try to maintain that everything is good end up in delusions, whether that is through succumbing to drugs or deception. Both users end up in an altered state of consciousness with their ability to deal with reality impaired. We must guard our hearts, not only from the blatant evils, but also from the darkness that comes to us as light.

²² "The eye is the lamp of the body; so if your eye is clear [spiritually perceptive], your whole body will be full of light [benefiting from God's precepts]. ²³ But if your eye is bad [spiritually blind], your whole body will be full of darkness [devoid of God's precepts]. So if the [very] light inside you [your inner self, your heart, your conscience] is darkness, how great and terrible is that darkness!

²⁴ "No one can serve two masters; for either he will hate the one and love the other, or he will be devoted to the one and despise the other. You cannot serve God and mammon [money, possessions, fame, status, or whatever is valued more than the Lord]. (Matthew 6: 22-24 Amplified Bible)

GOD's love through you should bring the light, which affords people a clear choice of good and evil, life and death, blessings and cursing. Allow GOD's love to offer people a moment of sobriety from the confusion of this world, so they can choose well. That is real love. As children of GOD, we abide in reality, which affords us a perspective of life based on truth. In a world oppressed by deception and lies, we must boldly share the light of truth. There is a saying that the truth sometimes hurt, and this is true, but that is much better than lies, which can kill. We must look at the gospel of Christ as a prescription from GOD to the world, which if altered loses its power to save from the disease of death.

CHAPTER 12
RUNNING ANCHOR

We are "running anchor" in the human race. If you are not familiar with the phrase "running anchor," it refers to the last leg of a relay race in track and field events. The ones chosen to run anchor are considered the most gifted and equipped to secure the win. They are the ones most capable to make up whatever ground was lost by the previous legs of the race. To make sure we do not fail to secure the win, GOD Himself has come and provided us the Body of Christ to run this last leg. For strength, He has given us His flesh and His blood to consume and has filled our lungs with the breath of His Holy Spirit. The victory is ours! We just have to run.

YESHUA told the Jews who resisted Him that if the works and acts, which they had witnessed, had been done in Sodom and Gomorrah, they would have repented.

23 And thou, Capernaum, which art exalted unto heaven, shalt be brought down to hell: for if the mighty works, which have been done in thee, had been done in Sodom, it would have remained until this day.

²⁴ But I say unto you, That it shall be more tolerable for the land of Sodom in the day of judgment, than for thee. (Matthew11: 23-24 KJV)

YAHWEH gave instructions to Moses to have the children of Israel keep feast and festivals to commemorate His acts of deliverance, so that in the times to follow, His people would not forget His faithfulness. Those of this present generation find themselves at the culmination of the ages, having a full record of YAHWEH's works of love and faithfulness. Of all the generations that have been on the earth, we are the most privileged and the most accountable. Though we have not been eyewitnesses of what has taken place in the past, we have the report just as the Jews did to whom YESHUA spoke.

In addition to the current technology of the mass media, which can get a word around the world in seconds, we have been blessed with His amazing grace, and granted access to the throne of GOD to get our petitions answered, and the gift of the Holy Spirit for immediate counsel, comfort, and power. It's time to leverage all which GOD has granted us to fulfill the prophecies of our generation.

¹Blessed is he whose transgression is forgiven, whose sin is covered.

² Blessed is the man unto whom the Lord imputeth not iniquity, and in whose spirit there is no guile. (Psalm 32:1-2 KJV)

³ To appoint unto them that mourn in Zion, to give unto them beauty for ashes, the oil of joy for mourning, the garment of praise for the spirit of heaviness; that they might be called trees of righteousness, the planting of the Lord, that he might be glorified. (Isaiah 61:3 KJV)

⁹ But ye are a chosen generation, a royal priesthood, an holy nation, a peculiar people; that ye should shew forth the praises of him who hath called you out of darkness into his marvellous light; ¹⁰ Which in time past were not a people, but are now the people of God: which had not obtained mercy, but now have obtained mercy. (1 Peter 2:9-10 KJV)

¹³ And one of the elders answered, saying unto me, What are these which are arrayed in white robes? and whence came they? ¹⁴ And I said unto him, Sir, thou knowest. And he said to me, These are they which came out of great tribulation, and have washed their robes, and made them white in the blood of the Lamb. (Revelations 7:13-14 KJV)

¹⁰ And I heard a loud voice saying in heaven, Now is come salvation, and strength, and the kingdom of our God, and the power of his Christ: for the accuser of our brethren is cast down, which accused them before our God day and night. ¹¹ And they overcame him by the blood of the Lamb, and by the word of their testimony; and they loved not their lives unto the death. (Revelations 12:10-11 KJV)

If you have chosen to entrust your life in the hands of YAHWEH through the salvation offered in YESHUA HAMASHIACH, then these verses speak of your potential and destiny. This is the good news for all of those who are uncertain about their fate or unsure of their identity. It is time to shed popular religious ideas for the truth of GOD. The truth of the gospel seems like an impossible proposition, and that is why the Spirit of GOD tells us that the just shall live by faith. Salvation is only possible with the help of GOD. It is impossible to accomplish in your own strength. Many of the false doctrines that abound today come from men trying to make the gospel more reasonable, therefore easier to accept by those needed for their financial support or validating potential. Here is what Christ said:

"How can ye believe, which receive honour one of another, and seek not the honour that cometh from God only? (John 5:44 KJV)

We can't be ashamed to give our lives for something that will make us look like fools to the world. You must let it all go to gain the ability to see it all and hold it all righteously. We gain that ability by being born again with the eyes and hands of Christ. We become His anointed body in the earth. You don't have to wait until you reach heaven to begin experiencing the righteousness, peace, and joy, which prevails there. The bliss of heaven is the presence of GOD. The good news of the gospel *of Christ is that you can enjoy His presence now.*

> *22 Judas (not Iscariot) said to Him, "Lord, how is it that You will manifest Yourself to us, and not to the world?"*

> *23 Jesus answered and said to him, "If anyone loves Me, he will keep My word; and My Father will love him, and We will come to him and make Our home with him.* (John 14:22-23 NKJV)

AUTHOR'S TESTIMONY

Before being touched by the life of Christ, I existed but I didn't know what it meant to live. I did not have my being in harmony with the power and spirit which ordered the seasons which dictated how I should live. I didn't love myself because I didn't know who I was, nor did I understand the root of the things which compelled me. All of that changed when the light of the true gospel of Christ pierced the darkness of my soul. The record of the Apostle John accounts Christ professing that He made all things. Since Christ made all things, He knows the purpose of all things that have been made and when I was ready to listen, He explained to me why I was made and what my life meant. Now I no longer walk in darkness where my ignorance was exploited by Satan, the enemy of mankind and all of creation. The gospel of Christ is the way back to the life which was stolen in the garden of Eden. No amount of wealth or pleasures in the world can restore the richness of the life which was loss in disobedience to GOD. Christ has come and given His life as an inheritance to those who are willing to lay down their disconnected existence to accept a life directly connected to the Creator. Through this new connection to GOD my soul now overflows with living waters capable of turning the deserts in my life to lush gardens. Now I wake up everyday to the counsel of GOD's love which leads me to live in harmony with His purposes and seasons. I have a peace which passes understanding because I live trusting the Word of my Father GOD instead of my own feelings and limited perspective. If GOD gave His life for me when I was living in ignorance and seeking my own way, how much more will He abound for me now that I am bringing my questions to Him to know His will for my life. The gospel of Christ is the only thing that makes sense of this world because it is Truth. As I share what I have learned of Christ by His word and spirit, I pray this book brings new life to you. Please get a copy of my first book: "True Heritage: Recovering From Spiritual Identity Theft". It helps to re-establish our root identity as children of GOD.

By His grace,

D.L. Fuller

CPSIA information can be obtained
at www.ICGtesting.com
Printed in the USA
BVHW041450301120
594526BV00009B/402